105088167

P9-BYY-458

A Ticket to
Japan

Tom Streissguth

Carolrhoda Books, Inc. / Minneapolis

Photo Acknowledgments

Photos, maps, and artworks are used courtesy of: John Erste, pp. 1, 2–3, 8–9, 13, 34–35, 42; Laura Westlund, pp. 4, 6–7, 10–11, 17, 24, 28, 32, 37; Josh Kohnstamm, pp. 5, 32–33, 36, 40, 41 (top), 45; © Michele Burgess, pp. 6–7; Harry J. Lerner/IPS, p. 7 (middle); © Diane Lyell, pp. 7 (right), 9, 18, 18–19, 25, 38, 38–39, 41 (bottom), 42, 43; © Bruno P. Zehnder/Peter Arnold, Inc., pp. 7, 31; Frederick Gonnerman, pp. 8, 11, 16, 17, 20 (top), 23 (bottom); Reuters/Corbis–Bettmann, p. 10 (top); AP/Wide World Photos, p. 10 (bottom); Kay Shaw, pp. 12, 19; AP Photo/POOL, p. 13; Corbis–Bettmann, p. 14; Leslie Fagre, pp. 20 (bottom), 21; American Lutheran Church, pp. 22–23, 24, 29; Stuart Atkin from *A Family in Japan*, by Judith Elkin (A & C Black), p. 23 (top); Kimimasa Mayama/Reuters/Archive Photos, p. 26; Susumu Takahashi/Reuters/Archive Photos, p. 27 (top); Bettmann, p. 27 (bottom); © Steve Kaufman/Peter Arnold, Inc., p. 28; Unicorn Stock Photos, p. 30; Archive Photos, pp. 34, 35; © Nelson–Atkins Museum, p. 37; International Society for Educational Information, Inc., p. 44. Cover photo of Japanese boys, Josh Kohnstamm.

Copyright © 1997 by Carolrhoda Books, Inc.

All rights reserved. International copyright secured. No part of this book may be reproduced, stored in a retrieval system, or transmitted in any form or by any means—electronic, mechanical, photocopying, recording, or otherwise—without the prior written permission of Carolrhoda Books, Inc., except for the inclusion of brief quotations in an acknowledged review.

Carolrhoda Books, Inc.
A Division of the Lerner Publishing Group
241 First Avenue North
Minneapolis, Minnesota 55401 U.S.A.

Website address: www.lernerbooks.com

Library of Congress Cataloging-in-Publication Data

Streissguth, Thomas, 1958–
    Japan / by Tom Streissguth.
        p. cm. — (A ticket to–)
    Includes index.
    Summary: An overview of Japan emphasizing its cultural aspects.
    ISBN 1-57505-127-3 (lib. bdg.)
    1. Japan—Juvenile literature. [1. Japan.] I. Title. II. Series.
DS806.S77   1997b   97–935
952—dc21

Manufactured in the United States of America
2 3 4 5 6 7 – SP – 04 03 02 01 00 99

Contents

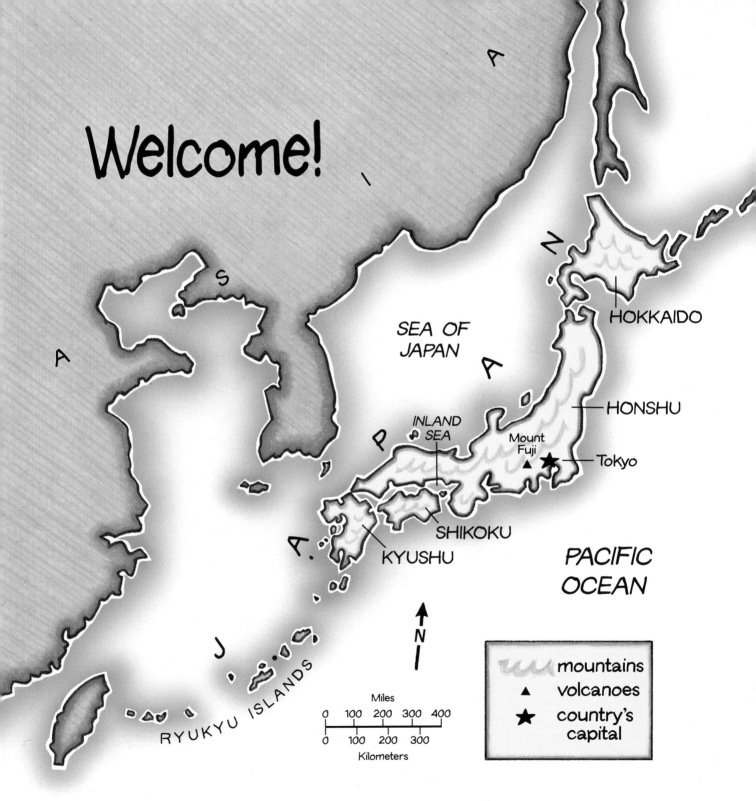

Welcome!

SEA OF JAPAN

INLAND SEA

PACIFIC OCEAN

HOKKAIDO

HONSHU

Mount Fuji

Tokyo

SHIKOKU

KYUSHU

RYUKYU ISLANDS

N

Miles
0   100   200   300   400

0   100   200   300
Kilometers

〜〜〜 mountains
▲ volcanoes
★ country's capital

Water, water everywhere. Japan is a country made up of 4,000 **islands.** Each island is a piece of land with water on all sides. Look at the map. The big piece of land to the west is the **continent** of Asia. Between Japan and Asia lies the Sea of Japan. To the east sits the great Pacific Ocean.

Map Whiz Quiz

Trace the outline of Japan onto a piece of paper. See the Pacific Ocean on the map? Mark this side of your paper with an "E" for east. Find the Sea of Japan. Put a "W" for west here. With a red crayon color in Japan. Color the rest of your map blue—that's the water. These red areas are called islands.

Where are the islands in this picture?

5

Crowded Country

Where do people in Japan live? Mountains cover most of the land, so people live in the few places where land is flat.

Japanese cities are crowded—especially Tokyo. About 8,000,000 people live there.

Tokyo is one of the world's most crowded cities.

Bullet Train

Faster than a bus! A car! A speeding bullet!?! Well, not quite. Bullet trains take you from city to city. At 155 miles per hour, you'll get there fast!

In Japan, some people live in cities (left) *where there is a lot of car traffic. Some people live in mountainside towns* (above).

That means 35,000 people live in every one square mile. Imagine 50 people living in your bedroom. That's how crowded Tokyo feels!

Workers in uniforms and gloves help people onto the **subway** *before the doors close.*

Some volcanoes smoke and steam (left). Others, like Mount Fuji (facing page), are quiet.

Volcanoes

The mountains of Japan are actually old **volcanoes.** A volcano is a hole in the ground where melted rock can

A Hot Bath

The inside of the earth is very hot. Heated water comes out through a crack in the earth to make a spring. A **hot spring** is like an outdoor bathtub. The Japanese like to visit these springs to take a long, hot soak.

flow out. Some volcanoes spit, gurgle, and smoke. Others have been quiet for many years. Most volcanoes on Japan are the quiet kind. To the Japanese, the most famous quiet volcano is called Mount Fuji. From the top of Mount Fuji, people can see for miles and miles—all the way to the Pacific Ocean.

Danger!

An **earthquake** is felt somewhere in Japan every day!

Can you believe it? This rumbling of the earth can cause buildings to fall down. The Japanese make their buildings to move with the earth so they don't fall down as easily.

(Left) *Schoolchildren in Japan practice earthquake drills. Earthquakes can wreck a city* (above) *in several seconds.*

Giant waves are a danger on the coast. An earthquake on the seafloor makes huge waves. The great big walls of water are sometimes as tall as a house.

Trash!

Garbage piles up and pollution goes into the sky. But the Japanese are pitching in to help clean up their country. They recycle things like old newspapers, bottles, and cans.

*One Japanese **folktale** says that a giant catfish lives beneath the land. Once in a while, the catfish swings its huge tail and starts another jishin—or earthquake.*

11

The Japanese

Many years ago, the Japanese didn't want strangers from other countries to change Japan. They made a rule that no one could enter or leave Japan. One Japanese person could marry only another Japanese person.

When you look around your classroom, do you see many different faces? In a Japanese classroom, students see many different faces, too.

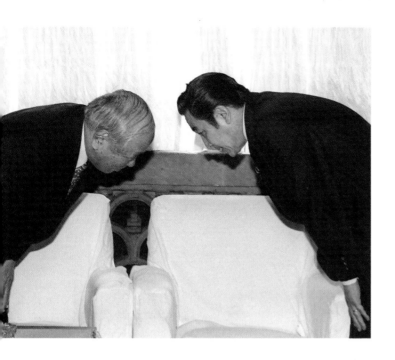

How do you greet a friend?
Japanese people bow to say hello.

The rule has changed now. But because of it, Japanese people tend to have the same eye, skin, and hair color.

The Japanese are very proud of their country. Nihon, the Japanese word for Japan, means "Land of the Rising Sun." Their flag even looks like a rising sun.

First People

The very first people in Japan were called
the Ainu. The Ainu still live in Japan on
Hokkaido. Can you find the island of

The Ainu (facing page) *like to remember their past. The clothes they wear help them to remember the first Ainu in Japan.*

Who else lives in Japan?

People from the countries of Korea, China, Vietnam, Brazil, and America also live in Japan. Some come to work. Others come to raise families. But no matter how long a non-Japanese person lives in Japan, they can't be Japanese—even if they were born there.

Hokkaido on the map on page 4? Some Ainu practice their old ways of life. They fish and grow rice. The younger Ainu go to Japanese schools and work in Japanese cities. The old Ainu ways are mixing with Japanese ways to make new **traditions.**

Japanese students talk with an American student.

Foreigners

If you went to Japan, you would stick out. A non-Japanese person may look different or speak a different language. The Japanese call the non-Japanese *gaijin.* In small towns where they don't get many visitors, people may be curious about gaijin. They'd probably stare and want to ask questions.

If the Japanese want to talk to someone who does not speak Japanese, they may use hand signals (above). Do you recognize this sign (right)?

*Paper screens in a
Japanese home*

The Home

Most people's homes in Japan are small.
Apartments in high-rises may have a tiny
kitchen, a little living room, and one or two

small bedrooms.
Brothers and
sisters pretty much
live elbow to elbow
with their parents.

Country homes
have few inside walls.

The Japanese use sliding paper screens to build walls wherever they want. That way a room can be made smaller or bigger as needed.

Tatami

The Japanese measure their homes by tatami mats. These mats cover the floors in the house. A room is usually four or five tatami mats. To keep the mats clean, the Japanese take off their shoes while in the house.

The Japanese sleep on soft, cotton mattresses called futons.

19

Dinner is ready!

The Family

Japanese kids spend most of the day at school. In the afternoons,

Try using these Japanese names for family members on your own family and see if they understand you.

grandfather	ojiisan	(oh-JEE-ee-sahn)
grandmother	obaasan	(oh-BAH-ah-sahn)
father	otosan	(oh-TOH-sahn)
mother	okasan	(oh-KAH-sahn)
uncle	ojisan	(OH-jee-sahn)
aunt	obasan	(OH-bah-sahn)
son	musuko	(MOO-soo-koh)
daughter	musume	(MOO-soo-may)
brother	onisan	(oh-NEE-sahn)
sister	onesan	(oh-NAY-sahn)

A Japanese family may have cake and other sweets to celebrate a birthday. How do you celebrate?

they go to an after-school activity. After a long day, they may arrive home hungry. Mothers spend part of the day preparing meals while dads are at the office. After dinner, it's time to do homework. There's a quiet space for children to study. In Japan doing well in school is very important.

School

Japanese children start school when they are six years old. Starting school means no more goofing around. Students must begin practicing to become an adult.

Sharing and getting along starts early for the Japanese. To make sure no one sticks out, boys and girls must dress alike. Students from the same school often buy their clothes from the same store. This store

22

Meet Kengo Tomita. Every day Kengo and his older brother, Daisuke, walk to school together. Kengo loves math, but not social studies. After a long day, his family has supper. Kengo takes a bath and does homework before bed.

carries skirts, slacks, blouses, and shoes to choose from. Students also each tote a leather backpack—black for boys, red for girls—to carry their school supplies.

Students shop for a school uniform (above). (Left) *Japanese schoolchildren meet before school.*

23

Using chopsticks can be pretty tricky— unless you grow up using them!

Food

The most important food to the Japanese is rice. They grow it everywhere. They even carve hillsides to make a flat field for growing rice. *Gohan*, the word for meal, actually has

Japanese restaurants have plastic models of food in their windows so you can see what you're ordering.

two meanings. It means rice, too.

To eat, the Japanese use two wooden sticks called chopsticks. They can be tricky business if you don't know what you're doing!

A Japanese Lunchbox

For lunch a Japanese person might bring a *bento.* This is a lunch that comes in a small plastic or wooden box. It may hold fish or chicken wrapped in rice. Or rice balls wrapped with seaweed. There may also be a salad and a cup of tea. What do you pack in your bento?

Indoor skiing—what fun!

Playtime

Where does your family go for vacations? To the beach? Skiiing? Many Japanese

Lasers blasting! Aliens attacking! The video game craze is big in Japan. Kids love to play after school in a video arcade or at home on a Nintendo machine.

can't get to the seashore or a mountain. But there's an answer— giant indoor playgrounds. A huge pool sits next to a sandy beach poured

Japanese kids love video games. Do you?

by dump trucks. Machines make snow that covers mountains for year-round skiing. What a blast!

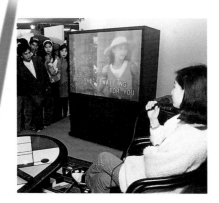

A girl sings karaoke. The words to a song pop up on a TV screen and music plays.

Lots of kids in Japan love to play baseball.

Sports

Baseball, or *yakyu,* is very popular among the Japanese. The rules are the same as they are in American

Soccer

. . . or *sakka* as the Japanese call it, is becoming very popular.

baseball. The only thing different is the size of the ballpark. It is smaller in Japan because land is hard to come by. Baseball is played everywhere from ballparks to playgrounds.

Sumo Wrestlers

Sumo wrestling is the national sport in Japan. At age 15, sumo wrestlers start training. They eat a heavy stew every day to help them get big. These strong wrestlers weigh in at 200 to 500 pounds!

These boys wear pads when they fight so they do not get hurt.

Martial Arts

Martial arts are more than just karate kicks. Martial arts—such as judo, aikido, kendo, and karate—come from Japan, China, and Korea. Each martial art has special kicks and punches to learn. Aikido doesn't use kicks or punches at all. People use turns and flips to get away from an attacker. It takes many years to learn these martial arts.

Two kendo experts practice their moves.

Dear Mom and Dad,

Konnichiwa! (That means "hello" in Japanese.) I'm having a great time. I've been meeting a lot of new people and learning tons.

Every day after classes we go to a special school where we learn kendo. (It's like sword fighting.) We use wooden swords, and wear metal masks, gloves, and cool body armor. I'm not very good yet, but I sure am having fun!

See you soon!

Writing

Japanese writing uses pictures, called **characters,** instead of letters.

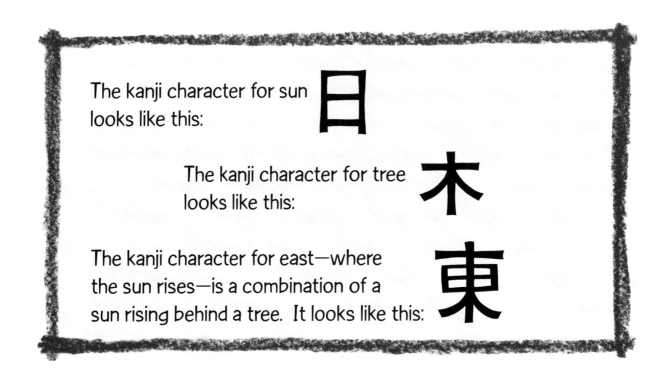

The kanji character for sun looks like this: 日

The kanji character for tree looks like this: 木

The kanji character for east—where the sun rises—is a combination of a sun rising behind a tree. It looks like this: 東

Kanji characters

Sometimes characters stand for a whole word. This way of writing is called *kanji.* Other times, characters stand for part of a word, or for a word sound. This type of writing is called *kana.* Here's an example. The English word animal written in kana has three characters—one for *a-,* one for *-ni-,* and one for *-mal.*

A man handles a tall puppet.

Puppet Shows

Bunraku is a type of Japanese puppet show. Bunraku stories are usually about Japanese myths and folktales. The people who move

Actors perform on stage.

while music plays.
The puppets are
three or four feet tall.

the puppets stand
behind the stage
wearing black to
hide themselves.
Another person
makes all the voices
for the puppets

A manga wall

Japanese Comics

If you like comic books, you'd like Japanese *manga.* The Japanese are famous for their comic book drawings. The weekly stories in manga are about superheroes fighting evildoers. The story keeps going each week.

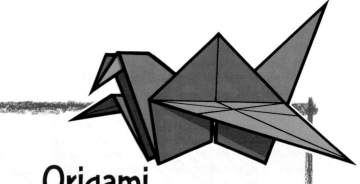

Origami

Could you imagine turning a flat piece of paper into a lion or a bird? The Japanese practice the art of origami, Japanese for "folded paper." Designs for origami can be simple or hard.

The Japanese make more serious art, too, like this painting.

Shibuya Station

Music and Meetings

The place to go for every kind of music in Japan is Shibuya Station. Shibuya Station is a section of Tokyo. There you can find people playing jazz music, rock music, and folk music all in the same neighborhood.

A popular meeting place in Shibuya is near a famous statue. The statue is of a loyal dog named Hachiko. As the story goes, Hachiko waited in this same spot every night for his master until he learned his master was dead.

Many Japanese kids like to pretend they are music stars. These kids are dancing to American rock and roll.

This man visits a sacred rock, called a kamisama, *in Japan.*

Religion

The oldest religion in Japan is Shinto. Followers of Shinto believe that all natural things have spirits, or *kami.* Volcanoes, trees, rocks, and mountains all have kami. The Japanese call them *kamisama.* (The word *sama* is used to show respect.) To pray to

A mother shows her daughter the tea ceremony.

Visitors to a jinja must pass through a gate like this one.

the kamisama people visit a *jinja*, or place of worship. People pray for many things, such as good luck in school or for a successful crop.

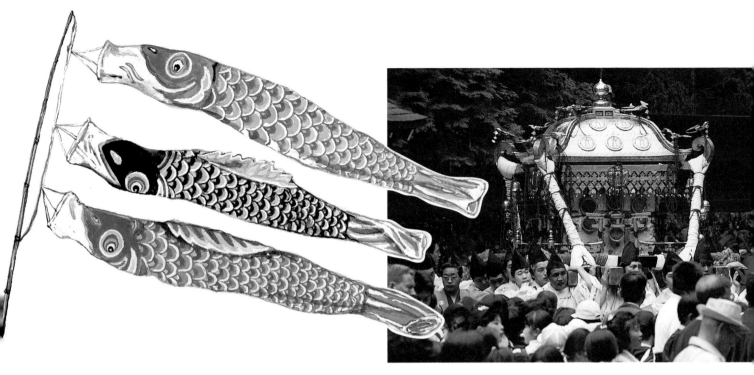

The Japanese often hold parades to help celebrate festivals.

Holidays

Imagine a special holiday just for children. In Japan boys and girls each have their own holiday. The girls celebrate their day, Festival of Dolls, on March 3. Fancy dolls sit on a shelf for everyone to see. Boys celebrate

Children's Day on May 5. Families fly kites shaped like fish, one for each son.

Firefighters' Festival

One of the most exciting holidays is the Firefighters' Festival. The firefighters balance on ladders. They set fires and then put them out. Ladder trucks line up and spray colored water into the air. It's quite a show!

New Words to Learn

A bullet train

character: Instead of letters, some languages, such as Chinese and Japanese, use a picture or symbol that stands for a whole word or word sound.

continent: Any one of seven large areas of land. The continents are Africa, Antarctica, Asia, Australia, Europe, North America, and South America.

earthquake: A shaking of the ground caused by shifting underground rock.

folktale: A timeless story told by word of mouth from grandparent to parent to child. Many folktales have been written down in books.

hot spring: Heated water from underground that makes its way through a crack in the earth's surface and forms a pool above ground.

island: A piece of land surrounded by water.

martial art: One of several ways of fighting and of protecting oneself. Martial arts include judo, kendo, aikido, and karate.

subway: A underground train that takes people to spots within a city.

tradition: A way of doing things—such as preparing a meal, celebrating a holiday, or making a living—that a group of people practice.

volcano: An opening in the earth's surface through which hot, melted rock shoots up.

Kites shaped like fish

New Words to Say

aikido	EYE-kee-doh
Ainu	EYE-noo
Bunraku	BUHN-rah-koo
Daisuke Tomita	DY-soo-kay TOH-mee-tah
Fuji	FOO-jee
gaijin	GY-jihn
gohan	GOH-hahn
Hachiko	HAH-chee-koh
Hokkaido	HOH-ky-doh
jinja	JIHN-jah
jishin	JIH-shihn
kamisama	KAH-mee-sah-mah
karate	KAH-rah-tay
kendo	KEHN-doh
Kengo Tomita	KEHNG-goh TOH-mee-tah
konnichiwa	KOH-nee-chee-wah
Nihon	NEE-hohn
Shibuya	SHEE-boo-yah
tatami	TAH-tah-mee
Tokyo	TOH-kee-yoh
yakyu	YAHK-yoo

More Books to Read

Brenner, Barbara and Julia Takaya. *Chibi: A True Story from Japan.* New York: Clarion Books, 1996.

Souza, D.M. *Powerful Waves.* Minneapolis: Carolrhoda Books, 1992.

Elkin, Judith. *A Family in Japan.* Minneapolis: Lerner Publications Company, 1987.

Haskins, Jim. *Count Your Way Through Japan.* Minneapolis: Carolrhoda Books, 1987.

Littlefield, Holly. *Colors of Japan.* Minneapolis: Carolrhoda Books, 1997.

Mayamoto, TadaTames. *Papa and Me.* Minneapolis: Carolrhoda Books, 1994.

Tames, Richard. *Passport to Japan.* New York: Franklin Watts, 1994.

Tompert, Ann. *Bamboo Hats and a Rice Cake.* New York: Crown Publishers, 1993.

New Words to Find